Contents

Comic
Cosmos

Why did the cow get into the rocket? Because it wanted to go to the moooooooon.

Boy to dad:
Do you know what an eclipse is, Dad?
Dad: No, son.

Why did the moon
not want any dinner?
Because it was full.

What is an astronaut's
favourite food?
Mars bars.

Why is there a 'K'
at the end of the word
'dark' and not a 'C'?
**Because you can't
'C' in the dark!**

Did you hear about
the angry astronauts?
**They just needed
a little space!**

What's an astronaut's
favourite key on
the keyboard?
The space bar.

How does the
moon cut its hair?
Eclipse it.

Ocean
Howlers

What did one shark say
to the other shark?
**This clownfish
tastes funny.**

Why did the shark cross
the Great Barrier Reef?
To get to the other tide!

What do you call more than one octopus? A nightmare to shake hands with!

Why do seagulls fly over the sea? Because if they flew over the bay, they'd be called bagels.

Why was the sand wet? Because the sea weed!

There were two fish in a tank. One fish turned to the other and said, **'Do you know how to drive this thing?'**

How many tickles does it take to make an octopus laugh? **Ten tickles.**

Silly School

Why is the obtuse angle always frustrated? Because it is never right.

Why is the maths book in therapy? To work out its problems.

Why did the
boy throw a
clock out of
the window?
**To make
time fly!**

Why did the boy bring
a ladder to school?
**Because it was
High School.**

Why did the
jelly baby go
to school?
**To become
a smartie.**

Did you hear about
the maths teacher
who fainted in class?
**Everyone tried to
bring her two!**

Pupil: Miss, I can't hand
in my homework.
Teacher: Why not?
Pupil: Because I ate it.
**Teacher: Why on earth did
you eat your homework?**
Pupil: Because you said it
was a piece of cake!

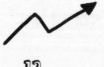

What do you do when
your teacher rolls
her eyes at you?
**Pick them up off the
floor and roll them back.**

Why doesn't the lollipop
lady work during the
summer holidays?
In case she melts.

What did the zero
say to the eight?
Nice belt.

What did the paper
say to the pencil?
You have a good point.

What did the science book
say to the maths book?
**Wow, you've got
problems.**

What do you call
a snake that is
good at maths?
An adder!

Did you hear about the kidnapping in class? **Don't worry, he woke up as soon as the bell rang!**

What did the pencil say to the rubber? **Take me to your ruler!**

Why did the kids study on an aeroplane? **To get a higher education.**

Knock, knock.
Who's there?
Broken pencil.
Broken pencil who?
Never mind,
there's no point!

Why is the corner
the hottest part
of a room?
**Because it's
90 degrees.**

Who is the king of
the pencil case?
The ruler.

Why was the strawberry
late for school?
**Because it was
stuck in a jam.**

Why did the teacher
write on the window?
So the lesson was clear.

Why was 6 afraid of 7?
Because 7 8 9.

Why did the teacher wear sunglasses in school? **Because her pupils were so bright.**

Why was the teacher cross-eyed? **Because he couldn't control his pupils.**

What do you do if no one laughs at your science jokes? **Keep trying until you get a reaction.**

Why is 69 so scared of 70?
Because once they fought, and 71.

What is the difference between a cat and a comma?
One has claws at the end of its paws. The other is a pause at the end of a clause.

Funny Furry Friends

When is it bad luck to see a black cat? When you're a mouse!

What do you call a dog with no legs? Doesn't matter what you call it, it still won't come.

What chases
caterpillars?
Dogerpillars.

What's a cat's
favourite colour?
Purrrrrrrple.

How do you tell a rabbit
from a gorilla?
They look nothing alike.

What is a
cat's favourite
chocolate bar?
A KitKat.

What did the dog say
when he got home?
I've had a rough day.

What do you get when
you cross a sheepdog
with a rose?
A collie-flower.

Any Body Laughing Yet?

HA HA HA

What did the cold say
to the chicken pox?
Catch you later.

What do you call
someone with no
body and no nose?
Nobody knows!

Doctor, Doctor,
I've got strawberries
growing out of my head!
I'll give you some
cream for that.

HA
HA
HA

When's the best time
to go to the dentist?
2:30 (Tooth-hurty!)

Why can't
your nose be
12 inches long?
Because then it
would be a foot.

Why did the
toilet paper roll
down the hill?
**To get to the
bottom.**

Why did the pie
go to the dentist?
**Because it needed
a filling.**

Knock, knock.
Who's there?
Moustache.
Moustache who?
I moustache you
a question, but I'll
shave it for later!

HA

HA

HA

HA

25

What do you give
an ant that's sick?
The antidote.

What do you give a
bird when it is sick?
Tweetment.

What did one
eye say to the
other eye?
**Between
you and me,
something
smells!**

HA
HA
How do you stop
sleepwalking?
Take a bicycle to bed.

Jolly Entertaining

What type of car does a Jedi drive?
A Toyoda.

HA HA HA

Why can't Elsa from Frozen have a balloon?
Because she will let it go.

Why did the iPhone need glasses? Because it lost all its contacts.

What musical instrument is found in the bathroom? A tuba toothpaste!

HA HA

HA HA

What do elephants watch? Elevision!

What do you call a droid that takes the long way around?
R2 detour!

How do you stop a bull charging?
Unplug it!

Which website do sheep like best?
Ewetube!

29

Why did the man put
the radio in the fridge?
**Because he wanted
some cool music.**

What type of
music does a
geologist like?
Rock music.

What sings
and grows out
of the ground?
Elvis Parsley.

HA

HA

Why does
Where's Wally
wear stripes?
**Because he
doesn't want
to be spotted.**

HA HA HA HA

What did the
drummer call
his children?

**Anna one,
Anna two,
Anna three,
Anna four...**

What does Willy Wonka
clean his teeth with?
Candyfloss.

31

What kind of photos do you find on a turtle's phone? **Shell-fies.**

What do you call a Teletubby that has been burgled? **A tubby.**

HA

HA

Why did the iPad go to the dentist? **Because it had a blue tooth!**

HA

Knock Knock.
Who's there?
Doctor.
Doctor Who?
Quick, get into
the Tardis!

Why do zebras
like old movies?
**Because they're
black and white.**

Why is Batman
always serious?
**Because he isn't
the Joker!**

Why does Peter Pan
fly all the time?
He Neverlands.

HA
HA
HA

How do you get
Pikachu on a bus?
Pokemon.

What is a clock's
favorite app?
TikTok.

34

Funny Food

What do you call it when a hen stares at a lettuce?
A chicken Caesar salad.

What do you call cheese that isn't yours?
Nacho cheese!

If there are watermelons, why aren't there earth, wind and firemelons?

HA

HA

Why did the banana go to the doctors? Because it wasn't peeling well.

HA

HA

What do eggs do for fun? Kara-YOKE-e!!

Knock, knock.
Who's there?
Banana.
Banana who?
Knock, knock.
Who's there?
Banana.
Banana who?!
Knock, knock.
Who's there?
Banana.
Banana who?!!
Knock, knock.
Who's there?
Orange.
Orange who?
Orange you glad **I** didn't say banana?

I want to tell you
a joke about butter?
But I don't want to
spread it.

Son: I think I'll wear
my banana suit today.
Dad: Why?
Son: Because I
want to look more
appealing!

How do you make
a sausage roll?
Push it down
a hill.

What do you
call a bear
with no teeth?
A gummy bear!

HA
HA
HA

What did the cake say
when it got in a fight?
**You wanna piece
of me?**

What kind of
crisps can fly?
Plain ones.

39

What did the cheese
say to itself in
the mirror?
Halloumi!

What did the wedding
cake say at the party?
**Pass me a tissue,
I'm in tiers!**

HA

HA

Why does
cheese sit beside
the phone all day?
**In case onion
rings!**

HA

Why should you always knock on the fridge door before opening it?
To make sure there isn't a salad dressing!

Knock, knock!
Who's there?
Lettuce.
Lettuce who?
Lettuce in, we're freezing!

Why was the cheese sad?
Because it was blue.

What is fast and crispy and flies into space?
A rocket chip!

HA

What is a leopard's favourite Irish vegetable?
Leoprochaun.

HA

HA

What did the ship's captain say when he saw a lettuce in the waves?
Iceberg ahead!

HA HA

Did you hear about the loaf at the zoo? **It was bread in captivity.**

HA HA

What do you call a fake noodle? **An im-pasta!**

What food prefers to be left unwrapped? **Nude-les.**

What did one cupcake say
to the other cupcake?
You ain't seen muffin yet!

Why did the boy throw
butter out of the window?
I don't know. Why did
the boy throw butter
out of the window?
Because he wanted
to make a butterfly.

HA
HA
HA

What did one plate say
to the other?
Lunch is on me!

My friend said an
onion is the only food
that can make you cry...
but then I threw a
coconut at her!

HA

HA

Knock, knock!
Who's there?
Phil.
Phil who?
Fill me a glass
of water.

What does a unicorn
call its father?
Popcorn!

HA

45

What's worse than finding
a worm in your apple?
Finding half a worm!

Did you hear about the new
restaurant called Karma?
**There's no menu — you get
what you deserve!**

HA
@

HA

Why did the lettuce
go to church?
HA **Because the priest
said, 'Let us pray.'**

Knock, knock.
Who's there?
Pasta.
Pasta who?
Pasta la vista, baby!

Guest: Waiter! Waiter!
There is a frog
in my soup!
**Waiter: Tell him
to hop it!**

What's orange
and sounds like
a parrot?
A carrot.

47

What do you call two
rows of cabbage?
A dual cabbage way.

What did the egg say
to the other egg?
You crack me up.

HA
HA
HA
HA

A boy asks his father,
'Dad, are bugs
good to eat?'
His father says,
'That's disgusting!
Don't talk about things
like that over dinner.'
After dinner, the father
says, 'Now, son, what did
you want to ask me?'
The boy says, 'Oh, nothing.
There was a fly in your
soup, but now it's gone.'

HA
HA
HA

Potty People

My friend got crushed
by a pile of books!
She only had her
shelf to blame.

HA
HA
HA

What's a
photographer's
favourite game?
Snap!

Knock, knock.
Who's there?
Says.
Says who?
Says me!

Why did the robber wear blue gloves? Because he didn't want to be caught red-handed!

Why did the one-handed man cross the road? To get to the second-hand shop.

What do you call a row of men waiting to get their hair cut? A barber queue!

HA
HA
HA

Why did the policeman
take his bed to the
police station?
Because he was
working undercover!

Why do actors
break their legs?
Because every
play has a cast!

HA
HA

What do
pirates say
when they burp?
Parrrrrrrrrdon!

What sits at the
bottom of the sea
and twitches?
A nervous wreck!

HA

HA

HA

What does a
pirate say when
he turns 80?
Argghh m'atey.

Did you hear about the
thief who stole a calendar?
He got 12 months!

53

Did you hear about
the dancer who fell
through the floor?
**It was just a stage
she was going
through.**

HA
HA

HA

HA

HA

What did the police officer
say to their belly button?
You're under a vest!

What do you call it
when a thief robs a
stationery store?
A rubbery.

Knock, knock.
Who's there?
Nana.
Nana who?
Nana your business!

What do you call an underwater spy? **James Pond.**

What do you call a man with an eraser on his foot? **Roberto.**

Why did the child walk across the playground?
To get to the other slide.

What do you call Postman Pat when he retires?
Pat.

HA
HA
HA

Why couldn't the ship's crew play cards?
Because the captain was on the deck.

Why do spies never parp in their beds? **They don't want to blow their cover.**

What do you call a grandmother on social media? **Instagran.**

HA HA HA

HA HA HA

What do you call a person with carrots in their ears? **Anything you want, they can't hear you!**

Why can't pirates
learn the alphabet?
**Because they get
stuck at 'C'!**

HA
HA
HA

Why don't pirates shower
before they walk the plank?
**Because they'll just wash
up on shore later.**

HA HA

Why did the chicken
cross the road?
**To get to the
fool's house.**
Knock, knock.
Who's there?
You are, fool!

Will you remember
me in 6 seconds?
Yes.
Will you remember
me in 6 minutes?
Yes.
Will you remember
me in 6 hours?
Yes.
Will you remember
me in 6 years?
Yes.
Knock! Knock!
Who's there?
You've forgotten
me already!

Animals
Antics

One monkey jumps into a bath. It says, 'Ooh ooh ah ah!' **The other says, 'Put in some cold water!'**

Why did the sloth cross the road? **To get to the other siiiiiiiiiiiiiiiiiiiiiiiiide.**

What do you call a
dolphin with no fin?
A dol.

How do you know if there's
an elephant under your bed?
Your head hits the ceiling.

Two snakes were
slithering through the grass.
Snake 1: 'Are we poisonous?'
Snake 2: 'No, we aren't.'
Snake 1: 'That's good!
I've just bitten my tongue.'

Pretend you're in the jungle and a crocodile is after you. What do you do?
Stop pretending!

Why do elephants hate penguins?
Because they can't get the wrappers off!

What did the lion say when he lost all his money?
I'm so paw!

What do
you call a
grizzly bear
in the rain?
**A drizzly
bear!**

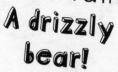

What did bear say to
his friends who were
waiting for him?
Please bear with me!

What happened to
the cheetah after
he had a bath?
**He came out
spotless!**

What's a crocodile's
favourite game?
Snap!

Why did the frog
go to the hospital?
**Because he needed
a hoperation.**

What kind of key
opens a banana?
A monkey.

What do you get if
you put an alligator
in a vest?
An investigator!

What do you call
an elephant in a
phone box?
Stuck!

What's a
unicorn's
favourite
hairstyle?
A ponytail!

What happens
when you cross
a porcupine with
a balloon?
POP!

What goes black,
white, black,
white?
**A penguin rolling
down a hill.**

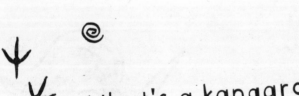

What's a kangaroo's
favourite season?
Spring!

Knock, Knock!
Who's there?
Who.
Who who?
Is there an owl in here?

Two ducks walking together.
One duck says to the other
duck behind, 'We're going
to be late. Could you walk
a little bit quacker?'

What do you call a
villainous crocodile?
A crookodile!

Why are frogs so happy?
They eat whatever bugs them.

Why do giraffes have such long necks?
Because their feet smell!

Why can't big cats take tests?
Because there are too many cheetahs.

68

Why do you never see
an owl when it's raining?
**Because it's too
wet to whoo!**

What goes ach-woooo,
ach-woooo, ach-woooo?
A wolf sneezing.

What is a mouse's
favourite game?
Hide and squeak!

Riddle in the Middle

Riddle me this...
What is taller when it's younger and shorter when it's older?
A candle.

Riddle me this...
If a yellow house is made of yellow bricks and a blue house is made of blue bricks, what is a greenhouse made of?
Glass.

Riddle me this...
There is a house with four girls in it. Grace is cleaning, Emma is playing chess, Lyla is reading. Where is Mya?

Playing chess with Emma – you need two people to play!

Riddle me this...
There's a boat full of people but there isn't a single person on board – how?

Everyone was married.

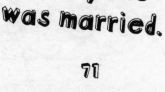

Riddle me this...
I weigh nothing, but you can still see me. If you put me in a bucket, I make it lighter. What am I?
A hole!

Riddle me this...
There are ten cats on a boat and one jumps off. How many cats are left?
None, they were all copy cats!

Riddle me this...
What five-letter word
becomes shorter if you
add two letters to it?
'Short' (add 'er')!

Riddle me this...
What question
can you never
answer 'yes' to?
**What does
'n-o' spell?**

Ticklesome Transport

Did you hear about the magic tractor? **It turned into a field.**

What happens to an illegally parked frog? **It gets toad.**

74

What wobbles as it flies?
A jellycopter.

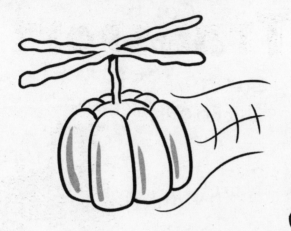

What do you call a train
loaded with toffee?
A chew-chew train.

Why did the girl smear
fruit on the road?
To make a traffic jam!

Knock, knock!
Who's there?
Cargo.
Cargo who?
Car go beep, beep,
vroom, vroom!

Why did the bus
look away?
Because the traffic
light was changing.

What's the fastest
part of a car?
The dashboard.

HA
HA

What do you call a
train that has a cold?
Achoo-achoo train.

HA
HA

A man took his old
bicycle to the scrapyard,
then the bicycle asked him,
'Can't you
recycle me?'

Eye-rollers and Groaners

What do you call a dear with no eyes?
No idea.

What do you call a dear with no eyes and no legs?
Still no idea!

HA
HA
HA

What is black and white
and red all over?
A newspaper.

A man walked
into a bar...
Ouch!

Knock, knock.
Who's there?
Surely.
Surely who?
Surely you know
my name by now.

Have you heard the
joke about the bin?
It's rubbish!

Why was the boy
running around his bed?
**He wanted to catch
up on his sleep.**

Knock, knock.
Who's there?
Avenue.
Avenue who?
Avenue learned
my name yet?

Why did the chicken cross the road? **To get some eggs-ercise!**

Did you hear about the man who invented 'knock, knock' jokes? **He won the no bell prize.**

Knock, knock! **Who's there?** I did ap. **I did ap who?** You did a poo? Oh dear!

HA HA HA HA

Knock, knock!
Who's there?
Boo.
Boo who?
No need to be sad,
it's just a joke.

Why did the cow
cross the road?
**To get to the
udder side.**

Knock, knock!
Who's there?
Will.
Will who?
Will you just
open the door?

Knock, knock!
Who's there?
Little old lady.
Little old lady who?
I didn't know you
could yodel!

How do you
keep a fool
in suspense?
I don't know.
Well, I'll tell
you later!

Knock, knock.
Who's there?
Watson.
Watson who?
What's on TV?

83

What did the doctor say to the curtains? **Pull yourself together!**

Why didn't the frog borrow the library book? **Because he'd already read-it read-it read-it!**

Knock, knock! **Who's there?** Interrupting cow. Interrupting cow wh— **MOOOOOO!**

84

Knock, Knock!
Who's there?
Candice.
Candice who?
Candice door open?

The past, present and future walked into a party. **It was tense.**

What did the envelope say to the stamp? **Stick with me and we'll go places!**

 85

Comedy

HA HA HA

Clothes

What did the left shoe say to the right shoe?
You're my sole mate.

What did the duck wear for the wedding?
A duxedo.

What did the dragon wear to the disco? **Hot pants.**

What do you call two banana skins on the floor? **A pair of slippers.**

Why can't elephants go in the swimming pool? **Because they don't have swimming trunks.**

HA

HA

What do you get if
you cross a sheep
with a kangaroo?
A woolly jumper!

What does a house wear?
**I don't know, what does
a house wear?**
Address.

What's leather
and sounds like
a sneeze?
**I don't know, what's
leather and sounds
like a sneeze?**
A-shoe!

HA
HA

88

Farmyard Funnies

What's a cow's
favourite dance?
The moo-nwalk.

Why are
turkeys so fat?
**Because they
gobble gobble
gobble.**

HA

HA

HA

What did one chicken say to the other chicken?

How are you cock-a-doodle-dooing?

What do you call a cow in an earthquake?

A milkshake!

How does a hen tell the time?

It looks at the cluck!

Where did the cow go on a trip? **To the moo-seum.**

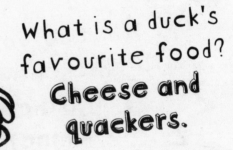

What is a duck's favourite food? **Cheese and quackers.**

What does the cow say when you're in its way? **Moo-ve!**

Why do milking stools only have three legs?
Because the cow has the udder.

HA HA HA

What do you call a chicken with no feathers?
Dinner.

What do you call a sleeping bull?
A bulldozer!

What do you call a cow with no front legs?
Lean beef.

HA HA

What do you call a cow with no legs?
Ground beef.

What is a cow's favourite chocolate bar?
Dairy Milk!

What's a cow's favourite night? **Moo-vie night!**

Why did the cake shop hire a pig? **Because he was good at bacon.**

Why did the scarecrow get a pay rise? **Because he was outstanding in his field.**

94

What do you call
a pig doing karate?
A pork chop.

HA

HA

HA

What did the mammy cow
say to the baby cow?
It's pasture bedtime!

What do
you get if
you cross
a chicken
with a fox?
A fox.

HA HA HA

What do you call a cow on a trampoline?
A milkshake.

What do you call a pig at a picnic?
Pig-nic.

When does a sheep go 'moo'?
When it's pretending to be a cow!

96

Knock, knock.
Who's there?
A cow says.
A cow says who?
No, a cow
says moo!

Why did the tortoise
cross the road?
To visit the chicken.

How did the
poorly pig
get better?
**It got some
oinkment.**

HA
HA
HA

97

Why did the
donkey cross
the road?
Because it was the
chicken's day off.

What do you call a
horse in clothes?
A horse.

HA
HA
HA

HA
HA
HA

HA HA Dippy Dinosaurs

Why did the dinosaur NOT cross the road? Because roads weren't invented yet.

What do you call a dinosaur with great vocabulary? A thesaurus!

Why can't you hear a pterodactyl going to the toilet?

Because the P is silent.

How does a dinosaur feel after a workout?

Dino-sore!

What do you call a dinosaur with no eyes?

A Doyouthinkhesaurus!

What do you call
a dinosaur's burp?
**A blast from
the past!**

Why can't
dinosaurs
talk?
**Because
they are
dead.**

Why did the
T-rex cross
the road?
**Because the
chicken hadn't
evolved yet.**

LOL-idays

Where do
parrots go
on holiday?
Parrot-dise

HA

HA

HA

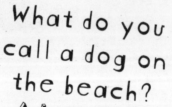

What do you
call a dog on
the beach?
A hot dog!

How many campers can
you fit on a campsite?
Ten(t).

102

What do you NOT take
on holiday?
An empty suitcase.

Why can't you run in a
campsite but you can ran?
Because it's past tents.

I wanted buy a
camouflage tent,
but I couldn't find any!

Where do sharks
go on holiday?
Finland.

What did the beach say to
the tide when it came in?
Long time, no sea.

Why do robots
need holidays?
**To recharge their
batteries.**

What do you call a snowman on a beach?
A puddle.

Where do bumblebees go on holiday?
Sting-apore.

Why are mountains the funniest place to go on holiday?
Because they are hill-arious.

HA

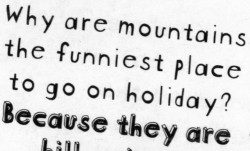

HA

HA

Sporting Chuckles

HA
HA
HA

Why was the
goalkeeper so rich?
Because he was
really good at
saving.

Why is Cinderella
so bad at football?
Because she
always runs away
from the ball.

106

What do you call a bike with no wheels, pedals or brakes?
Broken!

Why did the golfer bring a spare pair of socks to the golf course?
In case he got a hole-in-one.

Why did the footballer bring a bib to training?
Because the coach said they were going to practise dribbling.

What do you call a
pool with no pee in it?
An ool!

HA
HA
HA

How do surfers say
'hi' to each other?
They wave.

HA
HA
HA

Why is ice hockey better
than field hockey?
Because it's cooler.

Why do boxers make bad comedians? **Because their jokes are hit and miss!**

Why would babies make good football players? **Because they're very good at dribbling!**

HA HA HA

Why did the skater quit? **Because he got board!**

Why didn't the dog want
to play football?
It was a boxer!

Why did the bicycle not
stand up by itself?
**Because it was
two-tyred!**

HA

HA HA

HA

Why did the sheep quit football? Because he was baaaaaad at it.

Why are football pitches always wet? Because of all the dribbling!

HA
HA
HA

Wacky World

Knock, knock.
Who's there?
Jamaica.
Jamaica who?
Jamaican me crazy.

HA HA HA

What are the tallest buildings in the world? Libraries - because they have lots of stories.

What's the angriest
country in the world?
Madagascar!

Knock, knock.
Who's there?
Europe!
Europe who?
How rude!

HA
HA
HA

What is the only
county in Ireland
that won't sink?
Cork!

Knock, knock.
Who's there?
Kenya.
Kenya who?
Kenya open the door?

HA
HA
HA

Which city
do hamsters
like best?
Hamsterdam!

I've been working on
a Scandinavian joke.
**But I've not had time
to Finnish it.**

Nutty Nature

What's brown
and sticky?
A stick.

Why do bees
have sticky hair?
**Because they use
honeycombs!**

Why is grass very dangerous?
It's full of blades!

What room has
no windows,
no floor,
no walls and
no doors?
A mushroom.

What do you call
a boomerang that
doesn't come back?
A stick!

How do you know the
ocean is friendly?
Because it waves at you.

What do clouds wear under
their raincoats?
Thunderwear.

What do you call a
fish with no eyes?
A fsh.

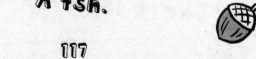

Why did the
mushroom go
to the party?
Because he
was a fungi!

What's the
difference
between a bird
and a fly?
A bird can fly,
but a fly can't bird.

What did one toadstool
say to the other?
Can you move over?
There isn't mushroom!

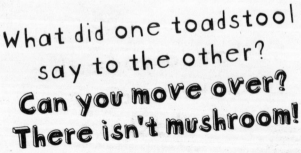

What do you call a fly with no wings?
A walk!

Why couldn't the bee go and play with his friends?
Because he was too buzzy!

What do you call a donkey with three legs?
A wonkey!

What did the plant
say to the rain?
Water you doing?

Knock, knock.
Who's there?
Leaf.
Leaf who?
Leave me alone!

Where do spiders
get married?
At a webbing!

I do!

What kind of tree
can fit in your hand?
A palm tree.

What did the big
flower say to the
little flower?
Hi, bud!

 **Spooky**

Sillies

HA HA HA

What does a skeleton say before dinner?
Bone appetit!

What kind of dog did Dracula have?
A bloodhound.

Why don't mummies have friends? Because they're too wrapped up in themselves.

How do you fix a broken jack-o'-lantern? With a pumpkin patch.

Do zombies eat crisps with their fingers? No, they eat the fingers separately.

What kind
of make-up
do witches
wear?
Mas-SCARE-a.

Why didn't the witch
wear a flat cap?
There was no point.

Why did Dracula
go to the library?
**He wanted to sink his
teeth into a good book.**

Why did the ghost
keep coming back
to the library?
She went through the
books too quickly.

What do you call
a magician's dog?
A labracadabrador.

What do you call a
witch at the beach?
A sandwich.

What do you get if
you cross an ice cube
with a Vampire?
Frostbite.

What do you call

witches who share
a house together?
Broom mates.

Why didn't the zombie
go to school?
He felt rotten!

Why did the vampire
go to the doctors?
Because he was coffin.

What room do ghosts
avoid in the house?
The living room!

What do you get if
you send a snowman
into a haunted house?
Ice screams!

What kind of streets do ghosts haunt?
Dead ends!

Why are ghosts bad at hiding their secrets?
Because you can see right through them.

How many zombies does it take to change a light bulb?
I don't know but you really shouldn't be in the dark with zombies!

129

Why did the skeleton
climb the tree?
**Because the dog
was chasing it.**

Which ghost is best
at goalkeeping?
A ghoul keeper!!

HA

HA

What do you call
a skeleton with
no bones?
A ghost.

What did the fisherman say on halloween?
Trick or trout!

How do ghosts like their eggs?
Terri-fried!

Hilarious Home

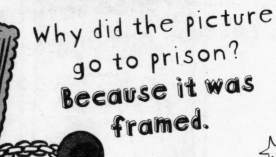

Why did the picture go to prison?
Because it was framed.

What do you call a can opener that doesn't work?
A can't opener.

How do you know if there's an elephant in your fridge?
Footprints in the trifle.

What's the difference between a postbox and an elephant?
I don't know. What is the difference between a postbox and an elephant?
I wouldn't want to send you to post a letter!

HA HA HA

Why did the toilet roll cross the road?
To get to the bottom of things.

Why did the teddy bear say no to dessert?
Because he was already stuffed!

HA
HA
HA

What should you do if you find a python in your toilet?
Wait for it to finish!

What did one wall say
to the other wall?
**I'll meet you at
the corner.**

HA
HA
HA

What did one toilet say
to the other toilet?
**I don't know, what did
one toilet say to the
other toilet?**
You look a little flushed.

What did the
smartphone say
to the calendar?
**Your days are
numbered!**

HA

HA

HA

What did the
fork say to
the knife?
**You're looking
sharp!**

Why should you
take a pencil to bed?
**To draw your
curtains!**

Christmas Crackers

What did one snowman say to the other snowman? Can you smell carrots?

Why does a turkey never eat Christmas dinner? It's always stuffed.

What is red,
white, red,
white, red,
white?
Santa rolling
down a hill.

What did one crisp
say to the other
crisp at Christmas?
Merry Crisp-mas!

What is the best
Christmas present ever?
**A broken drum – you
can't beat it!**

What's the best thing to give your parents for Christmas? **A list of everything you want!**

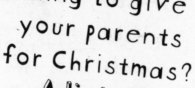

What do you call Santa on a trampoline? **A Christmas jumper.**

What do elves learn in school? **The elf-abet!**

Thank you!

Thanks to all the amazing comedians who shared their brilliant jokes to make this book possible! We're sorry that we couldn't fit every joke in, but hope that you continue to share the laughter!

Abigail, Magherafelt; Adam, Portaferry; Aidan, Belfast; Aidan, Crumlin; Aidan, Magherafelt; Aidan, Toome; Aideen, Claudy; Aideen, Magherafelt; Aimee Lee, Magherafelt; Aimee, Ballyclare; Aimeelee, Ballymartin; Aine rose, Magherafelt; Aine, Dromara; Aine, Magherafelt; Aine, Portaferry; Aisling, Castlewellan; Aiyana, Magherafelt; Alannah, Folkestone; Alesha, Comber; Alex, Magherafelt; Alex, Middletown; Alfie, Ballyclare; Alfie, Folkestone; Alfie, Spa; Alice, Limavady; Alice, Portaferry; Alyssa, Magherafelt; Amelia Rose, Derry; Amelia, Crumlin; Amelie, Belfast; Ameya, Londonderry; Andrew, Limavady; Anna, Ballyclare; Anna, Worksop; Annabelle, Crumlin; Annalise, Glasdrumman; Annie, Armagh; Annie, Portglenone; Aoibhe, Keady; Aoibhe, Toomebridge; Aoife, Crumlin; Arlo, Portstewart; Arthur, Crumlin; Austin, Bangor; Ava, Armagh; Ava, Crumlin; Avah, Magherafelt; Bella, Magherafelt; Benji, Newtownabbey; Braden, Crumlin; Braegha, Magherafelt; Bram, Crumlin; Brogan, Portaferry; Brooke, Derry; Cadhla, Craigavon; Caiti, Dorsey; Caitlin, Kilrea; Caleb, Annalong; Callum, Eglinton; Calum, Magherafelt; Calvin, Ballyclare; Caoimhe, Ballymartin; Caolan, Magherafelt; Cara, Maghera; Cara, Magherafelt;

140

Carli, Portaferry; Carragh, Magherafelt; Carson, Belfast; Cassie, Annalong; Cassie, Belfast; Cathal, Longstone; Catherine, Kilrea; Charlie, Carnlough; Charlie, Greenisland; Chloe, Glengormley; Chloe, Maghera; Chloe, Plumbridge; Christy, Coleraine; Cian, Longstone; Cillian, Magherafelt; Clara, Ballymartin; Cliodhna, Claudy; Cohen, Suffolk, Belfast; Coirle, Crumlin; Colleen, Crumlin; Conn, Seaforde; Connlith, Kilrea; Connor, Glengormley; Connor, Portaferry; Conor, Crumlin; Conor, Longstone; Conor, Portaferry; Cora, Portaferry; Corey, Crumlin; Courtney, Magherafelt; Daisy, Folkestone; Damians, Magherafelt; Dan, Worksop; Daniel, Annalong; Daniel, Longstone; Danielle, Portaferry; Danny, Armagh; Danny, Glengormley; Danny, Newtownards; Dara, Ballymartin; Dara, Magherafelt; Darcey, Belfast; Darcey, Derry; Darcie, Maghera; Darragh, Annalong; Darragh, Ballymartin; Darrin, Derry; Daryl, Magherafelt; David, Holywood; Devin, Kilrea; Diarmuid, Glasdrumman; Donacha, Downpatrick; Donnacha, Kilrea; Dovydas, Magherafelt; Drew, Longstone; Eabha, Magherafelt; Eamonn, Magherafelt; Eimear, Kilrea; Eimear, Magherafelt; Eimhear, Magherafelt; Eira, Holywood; Elijah, Ballymena; Ella-Rose, Magherafelt; Ella, Crumlin; Ella, Maghera; Ella, Trillick; Elle, Magherafelt; Ellie, Crumlin; Ellie, Kilkeel; Elliott, Greenisland; Eloise, Newtownards; Eloise, Folkestone; Elsie, Dundonald; Emilia-Rose, Brackneagh ; Emilija, Magherafelt; Emily, Annalong; Emily, Crumlin; Emily, Magherafelt; Emma, Ollerton; Emma, Portaferry; Ende, Portaferry; Enid, Dundonald; Eoin, Kilrea; Eoin, Magherafelt; Erika, Magherafelt; Erin-Louise, Glassdruman; Erin, Killyclogher, Omagh.; Erin, Magherafelt; Erin, Toomebridge; Ethan, Ballymartin; Eva and Riva, Cloughfern; Eva, Armagh; Eva, Holywood; Eva, Magherafelt; Eve, Holywood; Evie, Ballyclare; Evie, Banbridge; Evie, Magherafelt; Ezra, Portadown; Farrah, Crumlin; Farrah,

Longstone; Fiadh, Kilrea; Fionn, Kilrea; Fionn, Portaferry; Fionntán, Glengormley; Fionntann, Crumlin; Flynn, Annaghmore; Frank, Magherafelt; Freya, Limavady; Gabriel, Carrickfergus; George, Folkestone; Georgia, Carrickfergus; Georgia, Greenisland; Georgia, Portaferry; Gerard, Magherafelt; Grace, Ballyclare; Grace, Bangor; Grace, Dromore; Grace, Finaghy, Belfast; Grace, Magherafelt; Grace, Moira; Grace, Suffolk, Belfast; Hallie, Derry; Hannah, Downpatrick; Hannah, Greenisland; Hannah, Kells; Hannah, Newtownabbey; Harry, Greenisland; Harry, Kilkeel; Harry, Larne; Harry, Portglenone; Heidi, Portadown; Heidi, Portglenone; Henry, Ballycastle; Holly, Comber; Holly, Dorsey; Holly, Kilrea; Indi, Magherafelt; Isla, Kilkeel; Isla, Magherafelt; Isla, Scarlet and Bailey, Bessbrook; Issy, Portadown; Jack, Magherafelt; Jacob, Glengormley; Jacob, Magherafelt; Jaiden, Folkestone; Jake, Kilkeel; Jake, Lisburn; James, Bangor; James, Coalisland; James, Culloville; James, Magherafelt; James, Newcastle; James, Portaferry; Jamie, Kilkeel; Jamie, Magherafelt; Jarleth, Magherafelt; Jasmine, Annalong; Jaxon, Kilkeel; Jay, Portaferry; Jenna, Crumlin; Jessica, Belfast; Jessica, Cullyhanna; Jessica, Newtownards; Joe, Limavady; Joel, Kells, Ballymena; Joel, Longstone; Johan, Newtownabbey; John , Magherafelt; John-James, Annalong; Johnny, Crumlin; Joseph, Ahoghill; Josh, Greenisland; Josh, Ballymartin; Josh, Magherafelt; Joshua, Bangor; Joshua, Belfast; Joss, Broughshane; Jude, Crumlin; Jude, Newtownabbey; Julia, Magherafelt; Julie, Magherafelt; Kacper, Magherafelt; Kaine, Folkestone; Kaitlynn, Annalong; Kaja, Magherafelt; Kamil, Magherafelt; Karolina, Newry; Kathleen, Magherafelt; Katie, Bangor; Katie, Crumlin; Katie, Folkestone; Katie, Portglenone; Keelan, Portaferry; Keeva, Magherafelt; Kelsey, Longstone; Khloe, Annalong; Kindal, Folkestone; Kora, Kilrea; Kristie-Lea, Belfast; Kyla, Annalong; Lainey, Magherafelt; Lara,

Ballymartin; Laragh, Portaferry; Lauren, Magherafelt; Layla, Quigley's Point, Donegal; Leah, Glengormley; Lee, Longstone; Leita, Portaferry; Lena, Ireland; Lexi, Crumlin; Lexie, Portglenone; Liam, Glengormley; Libby, Folkestone; Líle, Magherafelt; Lily , Folkestone; Lily-Rose, Folkestone; Lily, Crumlin; Lily, Keady; Lilyanne, Belfast; Lincoln, Bangor; Lochian, Portaferry; Logan, Magherafelt; Luca, Bangor; Luca, Magherafelt; Lucan, Crumlin; Lucas, Ballyclare; Lucia, Crumlin; Lucia, Magherafelt; Lucie, Dungiven; Lucy, Crumlin; Lucy, Derry; Lucy, Kilkeel; Lucy, Kilrea; Lucy, Maghera; Lucy, Newtownhamilton; Luis, Magherafelt; Luke, Annalong; Luke, Castlewellan; Lydia, Ballymartin; Maddie, Kilkeel; Madison, Comber; Maggie, Middletown; Mai, Portaferry; Mairead, Magherafelt; Maisie, Magherafelt; Maison, Newtownabbey; Marc, Armagh; Margot, Folkestone; Maria, Donaghadee; Maria, Magherafelt; Mark, Kilkeel; Mark, Maghera; Mary-Kate, Magherafelt; Matthew, Kells; Matthew, Kilkeel; Matthew, Magherafelt; Matthew, Portadown; Matthew, Portaferry; Matthew, Randalstown; Max, Kilkeel; Max, Rathcoole; Max, Suffolk, Belfast; Maya, Magherafelt; Megan, Limavady; Mia; Miceal, Longstone; Michael, Crumlin; Michael, Magherafelt; Michaela, Toome; Miya and Mason, Craigavon; Miya, Kilkeel; Molly and Lucy, Ballyclare; Molly, Kilrea; Mya, Magherafelt; Mya, Ballyclare; Myah, Lisburn; Natalie, Belfast; Natasha, Magherafelt; Nedas, Magherafelt; Níadh, Glengormley; Niall, Crumlin; Niall, Head Road, Newry; Niamh, Kilrea; Niamh, Magherafelt; Niamh, Portaferry; Nico, Crumlin; Nilton, Magherafelt; Noah, Crumlin; Noah, Greenisland; Noah, Newtownards; Nojus, Craigavon; Norah, Belfast; Odhran, Crumlin; Odhran, Maghera; Odhran, Magherafelt; Oisin, Donaghadee; Oisin, Folkestone; Oliver, Carrickfergus; Olivia, Ballyclare; Olivia, Crumlin; Olivia, Folkestone; Olivia, Moira; Ollie, Comber; Ollie, Magherafelt;

Ooneen, Newtownabbey; Orla, Magherafelt; Orlagh, Omagh; Oscar, Kilkeel; Patrick, Dorsey; Patrick, Magherafelt; Patryk, Magherafelt; Paul, Crumlin; Paulius, Magherafelt; Phoebe, Ballymoney; Piaras, Kilrea; Pijus, Craigavon; Pippa, Middletown; Rachel, Kilrea; Rhia, Magherafelt; Riley, Derry; Robbie, Portglenone; Roisha, Magherafelt; Ronan, Crumlin; Ronan, Portaferry; Rory, Magherafelt; Rosey, Magherafelt; Roxanne, Folkestone; Ruadhan, Glengormley; Ruairi, Magherafelt; Ryan, Omagh; Ryan, Randalstown; Sam, Middletown; Samuel, Tynan; Sandra, Magherafelt; Saoirse, Annalong; Saorlaith, Magherafelt; Sarah, Banbridge; Sarah, Crumlin; Sarah, Holywood; Sarah, Kells; Sarah, Portglenone; Savio, Glengormley; Sawyer, Annaghmore; Scarlett, Crumlin; Sean, Ballymartin; Sean, Dungiven; Sean, Glengormley; Sebastian, Belfast; Senan, Castlewellan; Senán, Crumlin; Serena, Derry; Shane, Ballymartin; Shane, Maghera; Sienna, Derry; Siofra, Craigavon; Sofia, Crumlin; Sophia, Ballymaguigan; Sophia, Greenisland; Sophia, Kilrea; Sophia, Magherafelt; Sophia, Portaferry; Sophie, Annalong; Sophie, Ballyclare; Sophie, Ballymartin; Sophie, Glengormley; Sophie, Rasharkin; Sophie, Folkestone; Sorcha, Crumlin; Summer and Vicky, Newtownstewart; Taine , Longstone; Teghan, Ballymartin; Tess, Crumlin; Theo, Crumlin; Thomas, Annalong; Thomas, Magherafelt; Tiarnan, Dungiven; Toby, Comber; Todd, Kilkeel; Tom, Dungannon; Tomas, Magherafelt; Tomas, Portaferry; Úna, Coleraine; Verity, Ballymoney; Victor, Kilrea; Vince, Greenisland; Wiktoria, Kilrea; Zach and Rosie, Bangor; Zoe, Longstone; Zoe, Magherafelt.

With very special thanks to: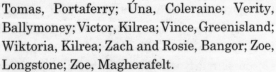